T0195963

# MAX AND COCOA'S ESCAPE

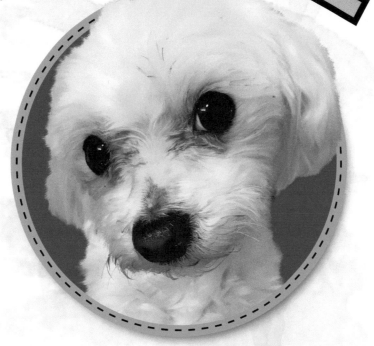

## ELSA PRADO

Archway Publishing books may be ordered through booksellers or by contacting:

Archway Publishing
1663 Liberty Drive
Bloomington, IN 47403
www.archwaypublishing.com
844.669.3957

ISBN: 978-1-4808-9715-1 (sc)
ISBN: 978-1-4808-9716-8 (e)

Print information available on the last page.

Archway Publishing rev. date: 11/27/2020

4720 W 99th St
Oak Lawn, Il 60453
(708) 557-5073
elsaprado@comcast.net

# Dedication:

For all fur-babies, that are part of the family. Although you don't speak you are unconditional love and emotional support. In your eyes, we see pure love.

# Max is Born

This is a story of a girl named Lilly and how she got her two dogs; Max and Cocoa. But then there is an escape that could cost them their lives. Come with me on this journey and we will go to the be beginning when Max was born.

For many years Lilly wanted a dog but she could not have one because her mom was working from home. Lilly was now in college and could now get the dog she always wanted. Lilly found a breeder of Maltese dogs and when she went to see her, she had a Maltese that was due to have a litter.

Soon Lilly got the call from the breeder and let her know that she could pick one of the five in the litter. Lilly made a special trip to pick her dog and picked the one that went straight to her.

When Lilly came home, she was sad and disappointed. Lilly explained to her mom that Max her new puppy would have to nurse with his mommy first and then she could bring Max home.

Lilly counted the days and received pictures from the breeder in anxious anticipation. When that weekend came, and it was time to pick up Max. Lilly went with her mom and came home with the most adorable white ball of fur you could ever imagine.

Max had a button nose and wide brown eyes and he just whimpered. They could not avoid feeling sad that Max was being separated from his mommy. Lilly was ready to be Max's new mommy and her mom gamma.

Max was so tiny he fit in Lilly's palm. He was very playful and joyful with everyone he met. Lilly was not really allowed to have Max at her college apartment but somehow got him there anyway. Max was so adorable his vet called him the Brad Pitt of dogs. Before anyone could realize time passed quickly and the years had passed with Max being the center of attention.

# Lilly Gets Married

Lilly had gotten engaged and was now getting married. Max was decked out in his tuxedo and looked dashing.

The photographer had taken spectacular pictures of the big day. The wedding couple went off on their honeymoon and Max stayed with his gamma. Max is the first gran-pup and his gamma would take him out everywhere. Shortly after Lilly got married, Lilly's husband wanted a dog too. So, they both decided that it might be a clever idea to investigate getting one plus they wanted a playmate for Max. Prior to this Max had been spending lots of time with his gamma.

Lilly and her husband Tom went looking to find different options. They chose to adopt this time since there are so many dogs in need of a home. They fell in love with a Corgi with stubby legs and a huge tail that he wagged around hitting everything in his path.

This adorable brown Corgi had been brought to a shelter after he had been found abandoned and left by his owners that no longer wanted him. The shelter told Lilly he did have some issues and suffered from some attention disorder and anxiety. However, Lilly and Tom felt that with lots of love and a loving home they could give this brown-eyed pup all the love and care he needed. Lilly and Tom named him Cocoa.

With the dark chocolate fur that he had and a long pink tongue that hung out from the side of his face, there was no way to say no to all the cuteness that Cocoa has. Lilly and Tom adopted Cocoa and brought him home to meet his new brother Max.

Lilly and Tom were not sure how Max would react but were ready to make it work. They both were adding to the family excited that this puppy would not suffer like he had suffered with the earlier owners. They were now the proud parents of Cocoa.

# Max Meets Cocoa

Lilly and Tom came home with their new baby pup Cocoa. Now it was time to introduce Cocoa to Max. Max was not happy to see Cocoa and Cocoa not thrilled to meet Max. Things did not go how Lilly and Tom had expected. They both were barking at each other and had to be kept from each other in separate rooms. There were concerns for the safety and well-being of both pups since Max was male alpha dog and was being territorial.

However, Max was smaller than Cocoa. With Cocoa having some Labrador mix in him he was larger than Max and could potentially hurt Max. It did take working with them and giving Cocoa lots of love since Cocoa had a history of being abused in the past. With determination and lots of love Cocoa started to improve and his trainers started telling Lilly that he was learning and more open to learn in his training classes. Cocoa has a bit of wildness to him; he does not pay attention very well and does do silly things that could get him hit by a car or hurt.

Eventually, Max and Cocoa started to accept each other and play with each other but let me tell you, as tiny as Max is all six pounds of him, he would pick on Cocoa. Cocoa on the other hand learned to relax and accept Max. Even though he would eat Max's bowl of food if Max were not watching at feeding time.

As time passed, they grew to be brothers is and they saw that they were both loved and that they did not have to compete for the attention they wanted. They each had tons of love and attention from the families on both sides.

But guess what? With two dogs in the house there was not much space and Lilly and Tom decided to buy a house with a yard where both Max and Cocoa could play and run around in.

# The New House

The family moved to a beautiful home on a cul-de-sac in the suburbs. Now Max and Cocoa had a huge yard to play in. Plus, the home was spacious with a lot more room. It was funny watching both learning to use the stairs, but they seemed to adapt and when Lilly's mom would stop by, both would welcome their gamma from the windows.

On one day that Lilly had to work she asked her friend that was staying with her to let the dogs out into the yard for a bit and then have them come back in. Tom also left for work that day. Just a few hours later, Lilly is getting a call from her friend that she forgot about Max and Cocoa and that they are gone from the yard.

Lilly called her mom to tell her that the boys were gone and that she was praying the police could find them

Oops

Lilly could not see how the dogs got out of the yard as it was fully fenced all around the house. She wondered if someone had gone into the yard and taken Max and Cocoa. Then she had a pit in her stomach thinking that they could get hit by a car, especially Cocoa, he had no sense to get out of the way without a command. How could Max and Cocoa even know their way home?

They were new to the neighborhood and still getting familiar. Lilly was afraid to even think she may never see Max and Cocoa again. The minutes were like hours and the hours were like days. Lilly could not help feeling angry with her friend. How does a person not remember two dogs that were led out to pee and then bring them back in as it was late fall and cold outside?

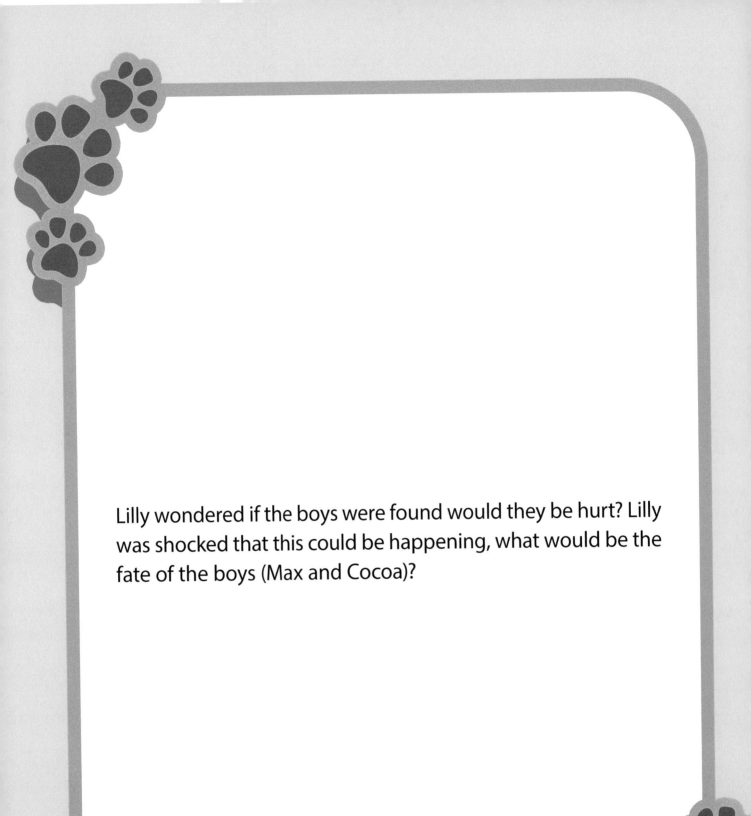

Lilly wondered if the boys were found would they be hurt? Lilly was shocked that this could be happening, what would be the fate of the boys (Max and Cocoa)?

# The Search

Lilly left her office and rushed back home from work. She was going to drive through the neighborhood to see if she could find Max and Cocoa. Tom also headed back home in disbelief.

Then suddenly, Lilly's mother in law calls. The police department is looking for Lilly. Since Lilly had not answered they called her mother in law who was listed as a contact.

The chip that Max had implanted worked and that had provided the police department with the information that they needed to reach Lilly. The chip that Cocoa had did not work so the police department was questioning who Cocoa belonged to. Lilly hurried over to the police department. She felt her heart pounding in her chest, the knot in her stomach and anxious to confirm that the dogs that were picked up from the street were Max and Cocoa.

When Lilly arrived, she was received by a female police officer. The police officer said that Max and Cocoa were walking in the street. It was a great relief to find out that the chip implant did work and that it led to a safe recovery for Max and Cocoa. As the officer said, "Without the chip implant information, the police department would have called animal control to pick them up." They could have ended up at the dog pound and then to an animal shelter.

After finding both dogs, Lilly could return home with them. Lilly called her mom to give her the good news that the gran-pups were returned safely. It turned out to be a huge lesson for the whole family since most of Lilly's family members have dogs. Lilly cried tears of joy.

However, the question remained, "How did Max and Cocoa get out of the yard? Lilly and Tom went out to the yard to figure out what could have happened….

# The Answer

They did a thorough inspection of the fence and found the gate was locked. They checked all the boards and found a loose board located towards the side of the fence. When they pulled it, they could see it was just enough room for Cocoa to fit through and with Max being smaller, Max followed.

Lilly told her mom she would not ask for favors anymore, the price of losing her boys was too high. Pets are a big responsibility and they form part of the family. Maintaining the safety of a pet is essential in case of a potential situation. Lilly did go back to have the chip implant for Cocoa fixed, she now knew the value of having her pets chipped.

You can say too she does not trust just anyone when it comes to the care of her pets and who can blame her? The love of a pet to us is unconditional. Pets offer emotional support to our families and fill our days with many interesting memories.

As you are reading this, can you think of any potential situations where your pet could have gotten lost? Let us keep that in mind so that we can be mindful in the care of our pets.

This story has a happy conclusion, some people do not get lucky and end up with loss. We can also help in making this a better place for our pets. Think about how you will make a difference.

The End

*Elsa Prado*

Author

Printed in the United States
By Bookmasters